Exploration Into CHINA

WANG TAO

new Discovery
B·O·O·K·S

Parsippany, New Jersey

First American publication 1995 by New Discovery Books,
an imprint of Silver Burdett Press.

A Simon & Schuster Company, 299 Jefferson Road Parsippany, NJ 07054

LIBRARY OF CONGRESS CATALOGING-IN-PUBLICATION DATA
Wang, Tao.
    Exploration into China/Wang Tao.
      p. cm.—(Exploration into)
    Includes index.
    ISBN 0-02-718087-5
    1. China —History—Juvenile literature. [1. China—History.]
I. Title.   II. Series.
DS706.W332   1995
951—dc20   94-28441
SUMMARY: An explanation of discoveries made in China

First published in Great Britain in 1994 by
Belitha Press Limited, 31 Newington Green, London N16 9PU
Manufactured in China

Editor: Jill Laidlaw
Designer: Andrew Oliver
Picture researcher:Anne Marie Ehrlich
Consultant: Frances Wood of the Chinese department of the
    British Library
Series consultant: Shane Winser, Royal Geographical Society,
    London
Map annotations: Hardlines

Photographic credits

British Library 2, 11 bottom, 12 top right, 13 top right,
19 bottom, 21, 24 bottom, 25, 26 bottom, 30, 34; **Bridgeman
Art Library** 35 bottom, 36, 37 bottom; **British Museum** 14,
20 bottom; **Comstock** 12-13; **E.T. Archive** 8 bottom, 10, 11,
15 bottom, 17 bottom, 19 top, 22 bottom, 23 top right, 24 top,
26 top, 28, 32-3, 35 top, 38 top left, 40 top left; **Mary Evans
Picture Library** 39 top right; **Werner Forman Archive** 9,
17 top, 38 bottom; **Sally and Richard Greenhill** 7 top right;
Sonia Halliday Photographs 23 middle; **Robert Harding
Picture Library** 3, 5, 8 top, 12 bottom left, 27 inset, 29;
Hulton-Deutsch 37 top, 40 bottom, 41 bottom; **Hutchison
Library** title page, 16 top, 23 bottom, 27 bottom, 42 top, 42
44; **Institute of Vertebrate Palaeontology Beijing** 7 bottom;
Popperfoto 39 bottom, 40 middle inset, 41 top, 42 bottom;
Courtesy of Brian Power 38 middle, 39 top left; **Museum of
Far Eastern Antiquities Stockholm** 7 top; **Wang Tao** 33.

Previous page:
Fishermen on the Li
River, Guilin, in southern
China. The Chinese
always say "the
landscape of Guilin is
the best in the world."

This page: **A** picture of
the Tiantai Mountains
taken from a Chinese
traveler's diary

Contents

An old farmer walks with his bamboo basket on his back. The majority of the Chinese population are farmers.

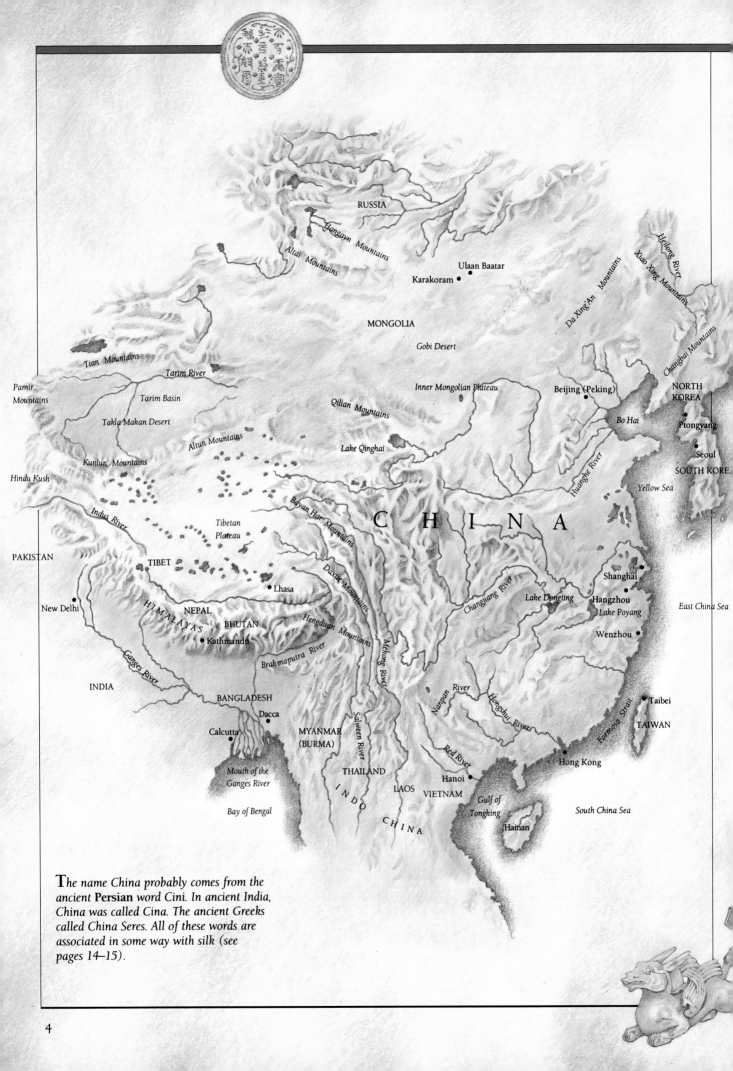

RUSSIA

Hangayn Mountains

Altai Mountains

Ulaan Baatar

Karakoram

MONGOLIA

Gobi Desert

Inner Mongolian Plateau

Tian Mountains

Tarim River

Pamir Mountains

Tarim Basin

Takla Makan Desert

Altun Mountains

Qilian Mountains

Lake Qinghai

Kunlun Mountains

Hindu Kush

Indus River

Bayan Har Mountains

Tibetan Plateau

Daxue Mountains

PAKISTAN

TIBET

Lhasa

New Delhi

HIMALAYAS

NEPAL

BHUTAN

Kathmandu

Hengduan Mountains

Brahmaputra River

Ganges River

INDIA

BANGLADESH

Dacca

Calcutta

Mouth of the Ganges River

Bay of Bengal

MYANMAR (BURMA)

Salween River

THAILAND

LAOS

I N D O

C H I N A

Da Xing'An Mountains

Xiao Xing Mountains

Heilong River

Changbai Mountains

Beijing (Peking)

NORTH KOREA

Bo Hai

Ptongyang

Seoul

SOUTH KORE

Huanghe River

Yellow Sea

C H I N A

Shanghai

Changjiang River

Lake Dongting

Hangzhou

Lake Poyang

Wenzhou

East China Sea

Mekong River

Nanpan River

Hongshui River

Red River

Hanoi

VIETNAM

Gulf of Tongking

Hainan

Taibei

TAIWAN

Formosa Strait

Hong Kong

South China Sea

The name China probably comes from the ancient **Persian** word Cini. In ancient India, China was called Cina. The ancient Greeks called China Seres. All of these words are associated in some way with silk (see pages 14–15).

1 Exploring China

The Story of China

Together with **Mesopotamia**, Egypt, ancient Greece, and India, China is one of the oldest civilizations in the world. Ancient China gave many important inventions to the world, such as paper, printing, the compass, and gunpowder. There are many things in your life that originally came from China, such as fireworks, chess, kites, umbrellas, and **porcelain** (see page 25). China has also borrowed things from other cultures, such as glass and tobacco. This book explores the fascinating history of the Chinese people and China's relationship with the rest of the world.

The People

More than 1.1 billion people live in China and the Chinese make up roughly one-fifth of the world's population. Although all of these people are Chinese, many also belong to **ethnic** minorities (such as the Uighurs, the Mongolians, and the Miao) and have their own languages, traditions, and customs. Some live in the border areas of China, such as the Jinuo and Wa peoples of the high mountains of southwest China.

A Huge Country

China is the third-largest country in the world and is bigger than the whole of Europe. Because China is so vast, it is divided into 22 regions, called provinces, that are controlled by local governments. These local governments report back to a central government in the capital city of Beijing (formerly known as Peking). A single Chinese province is often larger than a single European country.

Farmers make terraced fields so that they can grow crops on mountainsides.

The Land

If you follow the outline of China on a map, you will find that it looks rather like a chicken, with its head in the northeast and tail in the northwest.

The landscape varies dramatically in different parts of China. The Tian Shan and the Gobi Desert are in the northwest. The northeast reaches to Siberia, where the temperature can fall as low as −40°F in winter. This northeastern route was the traditional way Chinese people traveled to Russia, Mongolia, Korea, and overseas to Japan. The south of China is **semitropical** and has borders with the countries of mainland Southeast Asia. The mountains in the southwest of China join up with the Himalayas. The longest rivers in China, the Changjiang and Huanghe, both start in the Kunlun Mountains in the west and flow eastward to the Pacific Ocean. The coast of China runs along this ocean for 7,440 miles, and the major ports on the coast, such as Guangzhou (formerly Canton) and Shanghai, have been gateways to the Pacific Ocean and the rest of the world for centuries.

The Beginnings of Civilization

This map shows the locations of some of the earliest civilizations in China.

In the 19th century, Western historians believed that people traveled to China from Mesopotamia about 5,000 years ago. But **archaeologists** have now found traces of human activity all over China from all periods of time.

Peking Man

In 1929, a young Chinese archaeologist, Pei Wenzhong (1904–1982), found a seven-million-year-old human skull, which he called "Peking man." Peking man lived in caves at Zhoukoudian, a hilly area near China's modern-day capital of Beijing. We know that millions of years ago people made stone tools and used fire to cook and to protect themselves from the cold. Seven million years ago, Zhoukoudian was surrounded by rivers and **grasslands**, and wild animals lived in the bushes and forests. The early humans hunted deer in the forests and gathered fruit from trees to survive.

Yangshao Villages

About 7,000 years ago, there were many farming villages along the Huanghe River Valley. The people of these villages used polished stone tools, grew **millet**, wheat, and barley, and collected fruit from the forest and fish from the rivers. They kept animals such as pigs and dogs and made pottery jars to store their food. They decorated their pottery with beautiful patterns of plants, animals, and humans. We know from **excavated** human remains that when a person died he or she was buried in a public cemetery behind the houses of the village. Each village built a large central house for public meetings.

This is an artist's impression of a Yang Shao village. These villages were usually ruled by female chiefs. The largest building in the illustration is the village meetinghouse.

J. G. Anderson

One of the most famous foreign archaeologists to work in China was the Swede J. G. Anderson (1874–1960). When Anderson was young, he took part in expeditions to the North and South Poles. In 1914, Anderson went to China to work as a **geologist**. Later, he became more interested in archaeology. Anderson discovered the **Neolithic** village of Yang Shao in Henan Province and worked at Zhoukoudian, where Peking man was found.

These modern-day rice farmers grow and harvest rice in the same way as their ancestors did thousands of years ago.

Ricegrowing in the South

People in north China grew millet while people in south China grew rice. Chinese archaeologists have found a 7,000-year-old settlement at Hemudu near Hangzhou Bay, where wooden houses were built above the ground on stilts. The people of Hemudu were among the earliest rice farmers in the world and some of the objects they made from bone are beautifully carved with images of birds and plants.

The early inhabitants of north and south China are the ancestors of modern-day Chinese people. The people of these two areas had very different lifestyles and yet they traded goods with one another and learned about one another's culture. These people made beautiful carvings on stone, jade, and bones and painted their pottery with distinctive designs. Together, the early humans of north and south China created the beginnings of Chinese civilization.

This is the reconstructed head of Peking man. He had high eyebrows and a pointed mouth.

This bronze cooking pot is decorated with a human face and animal claws. It dates from the 14th to the 11th centuries B.C.

A 13th-century B.C. bronze taotie.

This Shang bronze was used to hold food during religious ceremonies.

Bronze Age China

The Bronze Age began in China in about 3000 B.C. It differed from the European Bronze Age because the Chinese did not make many bronze farming tools. They concentrated on making elaborate bronze objects for use in their religious ceremonies.

In about 1600 B.C. the Shang established their rule (called a **dynasty**) in the Central Plains (see map). The Shang moved their capital city many times and finally settled at Anyang, in Henan Province. They built palaces, royal tombs, and workshops for making bronze weapons and other objects. Many Shang **bronzes** have a distinctive two-eyed mask design called a *tao tieh*.

The Shang had many **colonies** and were frequently at war. In the middle of the 11th century B.C., the Shang dynasty was defeated by the Zhou from northwest China.

The green area shows where ancient bronze objects have been found.

Bo Hai

Xingtai

Luoyang • Anyang
• Zhengzhou

Yellow Sea

Central Plains

Hunan   Jiangxi

The Rise of the Zhou

When the Zhou overthrew the Shang, the Zhou king divided up the land and gave it to his close family and relatives. He gave them all the title of "lord" and gifts such as chariots, **textiles**, and slaves. Details of these gifts were often written on bronzes that were passed down from generation to generation.

The Zhou kings lived in their capital and traveled out to the country to worship the mountains and rivers in different seasons. At the beginning of the Zhou's reign, more than 70 states were given to members of the royal family to rule. These people later fought one another for land and power. In 841 B.C., King Li was thrown out of his palace by his own people, and they governed the country for the next 14 years. There was constant conflict between the Zhou and many minority peoples (whom the Zhou called "Barbarians"). The next king, Ping, had to move his capital to Luoyang in 770 B.C. because **nomads** from the west invaded the old capital, Gaojing.

The Shang and Zhou people liked hunting rabbits, birds, tigers, and rhinoceroses.

The Earliest Chinese Writing

Early Chinese writing has been found carved into bones at Anyang. Although there are some earlier **inscriptions** on Neolithic pottery, these bones show the earliest surviving example of the written Chinese language. Some of the words (called characters) carved into ox bones and turtle shells refer to religion (and so are called oracle bones) and some of them are historical records. If the Shang king wanted to know what the weather was going to be like, his advisers made cracks on a prepared animal bone, or sometimes several bones, using a heated rod. Then they read the cracks: *Tomorrow is a fine day, no rain. Tomorrow is not a fine day, it will rain.* The information was written on the bones and put away for future reference.

These Shang oracle bones (14th century B.C.) record a family history (above and below).

Early Philosophers

The Zhou dynasty survived longer than any other dynasty in Chinese history (c. 1100–221 B.C.). But the last 300 years of the dynasty's reign were very violent and are called the Warring States Period. From the seventh century B.C. onward, China was in a constant state of unrest. The Zhou kings lost control of the country and semi-independent lords and dukes fought one another to gain more land. Early Chinese **scholars** reacted to this situation by creating new ways of thinking about the world, called philosophy. New theories of philosophy and hundreds of different philosophical schools flourished.

The Philosophy of Confucius

Confucius (551–479 B.C.) was born into a family of **officials** in the state of Lu, in the modern-day province of Shandong. He admired earlier wise men and felt sad about the lost "paradise" of previous Chinese societies. He tried to restore old customs and ceremonies through his teachings. His pupils recorded his teachings, which later became the state religion of the Chinese government and were followed by every Chinese official.

This 18th-century drawing by a Japanese artist is based on the legend that Confucius was once Laozi's student.

Confucius's Rivals

Laozi (c. 604–531 B.C.) was the founder of the Daoist (or Taoist) religion. Laozi thought that nonaction is the best solution to any problem and that returning to nature is the Right Way to Live, or the *Dao* of things. Legend says that Laozi was traveling on an oxcart and a gatekeeper stopped him and persuaded him to write down his philosophy. Laozi's book has been translated into many languages.

Mozi (c. 479–381 B.C.) was Confucius' main rival. Unlike Confucius, Mozi opposed music and lavish ceremonies, such as elaborate burials. He hated war and believed in "love-all" —loving everyone regardless of their social status, age, or sex. Mozi had many students and all their writings were published under his name. Mozi and his followers were very interested in science and probably made the first kites.

This is the Daoist Symbol of the Cosmos. It represents a symbolic balance between the yin (dark section) and yang (light section) aspects of the world.

A later philosopher, Zhuang Zhou (c. 369–290 B.C.), refused to take any official government posts, preferring to live in poverty. He believed that people should respect nature and once dreamed he had become a butterfly. He then asked his students if they thought he was Zhuang Zhou dreaming he was a butterfly, or whether he was a butterfly dreaming he was Zhuang Zhou.

2 The Great Empire

The First Emperor

The Warring States Period ended in 221 B.C., when the Qin state in the northwest of China managed to unite the whole country. The king of Qin then became the First Emperor—Shihuangdi (259–210 B.C.)—of China, reigning from 221 to 210 B.C.

A map of the Qin empire at its height

A portrait (below) of the First Emperor, Qin Shihuangdi. The picture (left) illustrates Qin's soldiers burying scholars and burning their books. We can tell that this is a later drawing because books of Qin's time were written on bamboo slips, not on paper (as in the picture).

To strengthen his rule, Qin Shihuangdi ordered that all works of literature and philosophy were to be burned and 500 scholars were buried alive. He built lavish palaces, put up stone tablets that praised his achievements, and traveled all over China. Qin Shihuangdi believed that it was possible to live forever. He sent hundreds of young boys and girls into the sea to search for the magic plant of long life. But they all drowned and Qin Shihuangdi only lived for 49 years. He died while touring China and his death was kept secret for weeks, until the smell of his body was overpowering. Just four years after Qin Shihuangdi's death, the Qin dynasty was overthrown by a peasant uprising in 206 B.C.

The Terra-cotta Army

In 1974, a peasant digging for water accidentally discovered an army made of **terra-cotta** a few miles away from the First Emperor of Qin's tomb. Thousands of clay soldiers, horses, and chariots have now been excavated. They are all life-sized and have different faces, hairstyles, and expressions. Several pits containing clay soldiers surround the emperor's tomb because he believed that his terra-cotta army would protect his soul in the **afterlife**.

The four pits that surround the emperor's tomb contain the terra-cotta army—one pit alone contains 6,000 figures.

Qin Shihuangdi's Tomb

As soon as he became emperor, Qin Shihuangdi started to build his own tomb at Li Mountain, near modern-day Xi'an. It took seven million workers ten years to finish. The burial chamber floor was made of copper and the tomb contained a model of the royal palace with its numerous **treasuries** and precious objects.

The Han Dynasty

Liu Ban (256–195 B.C.), a low-ranking official of the Qin government, defeated all his enemies during the peasant uprising and established the Han dynasty in 202 B.C.

During the Han dynasty, agriculture developed rapidly and ox plows and iron tools were widely used. China became very rich and powerful. The Han emperors expanded their territory in all directions.

A *portrait of the Han emperor Liu Ban*

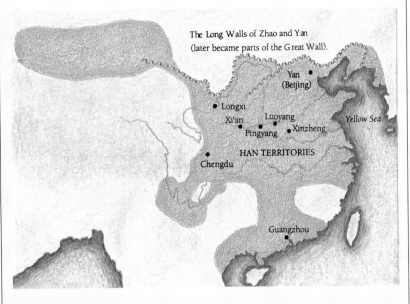

This map shows the extent of the Han empire at its height.

The Yellow Turban Rebellions

In the third century A.D., many popular Daoist sects (groups) rose up against the Han government and brought about its collapse. People belonging to the sects often wore yellow turbans around their heads, so their uprisings have been called the Yellow Turban Rebellions. China sank into a new period of unrest after these rebellions. Between A.D. 304 and 580, there were power struggles on the Central Plains, and on the northern and western frontiers many minority peoples established their own kingdoms.

This picture shows two craftsmen chopping and soaking bamboo for making paper.

The Invention of Paper

Paper was invented in China in the second century B.C. People started to use plants, such as hemp, to make thin paper. Before this time, people wrote on pottery, bones, stone, silk, wood, and bamboo. In A.D. 105 Cai Lun, an official of the Han court, improved the technology of papermaking and his name has been associated with papermaking ever since. Eight centuries later, papermaking spread to the Arab world and from there to Europe.

The Great Wall was not built entirely by the First Emperor. Some of it existed before him, but he did make it much longer.

The Silk Road and the Romans

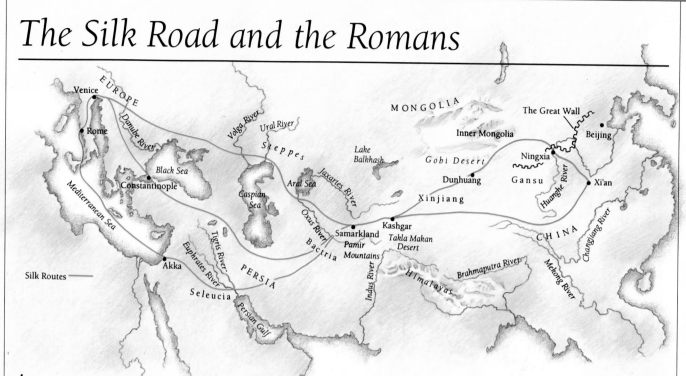

A *map of the Silk Routes. The illustration (bottom)
shows a camel caravan traveling across the desert.*

This eighth- or ninth-century painted silk was
discovered along the ancient Silk Road.

In the first century A.D., the Roman Empire was at the height of its power. It became fashionable in Rome to make clothes out of soft, transparent (see-through) silk from China. The price of silk was very high in Rome: The best Chinese bark (a particular kind of silk) cost as much as 300 denarii (a Roman soldier's salary for an entire year). Silk was brought to Rome in many different ways, but usually by land. The most popular route crossed the Gobi Desert, Bactria, and Seleucia before finally reaching Rome. This route was called the Silk Road. Often the silk passed through the hands of many traders on its way to Rome. The Chinese also developed a taste for foreign imports, such as glass, precious stones, perfume, linen, coral, and pearls, which all came from Rome and Egypt.

A modern traveler walks along the ancient Silk Road to Karakoram.

The First Chinese Traveler to Central Asia

In 138 B.C. the Han emperor Wudi (156–87 B.C.) sent his official Zhang Qian (died 114 B.C.) to seek **allies** to fight the **Huns** of the northwest grasslands. But the Huns captured Zhang Qian and imprisoned him for ten years. Zhang Qian managed to escape and return to the capital, Xi'an. In 119 B.C., Zhang Qian made his second trip to central Asia, this time with a team of 300 people. Zhang Qian brought back lots of information about central Asia and visitors from the Wusun tribe.

The people of central Asia and China had been trading with one another long before Zhang Qian's mission, but Zhang Qian was the first person to record anything about central Asia and its people. As a result of his mission, the Silk Road became even busier than before. Chinese silk and cast-iron objects were **exported** to the West, and grapes, walnuts, and **pomegranates** were brought into China.

The Rediscovery of the Silk Road

The Silk Road was buried for more than a thousand years. During the late 19th century, European explorers began searching for the lost cities and cultures of the Silk Road. The most famous of these explorers were Sven Hedin (1865–1952) and Aurel Stein (1862–1943).

Sven Hedin and Aurel Stein

The Swedish explorer Sven Hedin made four expeditions to China. In 1893, he crossed the Pamir Mountains and reached Kashgar, temporarily losing his sight because of the extreme cold and **mountain sickness**. During his second expedition in 1899, Hedin discovered the long-lost city of Loulan in the Takla Makan Desert. In 1906, Hedin traveled to Tibet and the Himalayas to study archaeology, the climate, and plant life. Hedin's last expedition, in 1927, was with many Chinese scholars to Inner Mongolia, Ningxia, Gansu, and Xinjiang, where they made many important archaeological discoveries.

Aurel Stein was a Hungarian-British archaeologist who made three important expeditions from India into China from 1900 to 1918. He mapped China and carried out archaeological surveys and excavations. During his second expedition Stein met Wang Yuanlu, a Chinese Daoist priest. He showed Stein a fabulous library dating from the fourth to the tenth centuries, which was hidden in the Caves of a Thousand Buddhas at Dunhuang.

Many beautiful images have survived from the eighth and ninth centuries from the Caves of a Thousand Buddhas at Dunhuang.

The Arrival of Buddhism

This giant statue of Buddha is 230 feet high. It was carved out of the side of a mountain in Sichuan during the eighth century.

From India to China

Buddhism was brought to China from India during the first century A.D. This religion was founded by Siddhartha Gautama, a prince born in about 560 B.C. Siddhartha lived in great luxury, but was unhappy with his life. When he was 29, Siddhartha gave up his wealth and left his father's palace to travel around India. He spent the remaining 44 years of his life searching for truth on his journey. He preached that the best way to find the truth was to **meditate** and to be non-violent and moderate in all things. The aim of the Buddhist religion is for an individual to reach a state of personal enlightenment by following Buddha's teachings. Englightenment is the name given to the state of mind people reach when they feel that they can see the true nature of all things.

A Popular Religion

Buddhism was very popular in China from the first to the eighth centuries A.D. In A.D. 68, the Han emperor Mingdi sent his official Cai Yin to central Asia to learn more about Buddhism after a vision of a golden figure appeared to him in a dream. The next morning he asked his ministers what the dream meant and was told that he had seen the Buddha—the god of the West. Cai Yin returned to Luoyang, the new Han capital, with images of the Buddha, Buddhist scriptures, and two Buddhist monks. They arrived in Luoyang riding on white horses, and the temple built for them was named the White Horse Temple.

Buddhists have carved and painted many images of Buddha. This is the famous seventh-century Longmen Grottoes near Luoyang.

During the sixth century, the emperor Xiao Yan (464–549) became a Buddhist monk and left his palace on three occasions to seek enlightenment. The government he left behind had to give large sums of money to Buddhist temples in order to persuade Xiao Yan to return.

This is a map of the canals built during the Sui dynasty.

The Grand Canal

The Grand Canal was an ambitious project started during the Sui dynasty (sixth to seventh centuries) (see page 18). More than a million people built the canal so that the transportation of rice and weapons between north and south China would be easier. The canal is 600 miles long and was the largest of its type until the 18th century when Europeans began to build commercial waterways on a similar scale.

Emperor Yang Di built the Grand Canal. Here he is shown traveling on the canal, followed by a large number of women and servants.

3 The Golden Age

The Center of the World

An artist's impression of a market scene in the city of Xi'an.

Xi'an

The Tang capital city, Xi'an, was designed by Yu Wenkai, and the building work started in 582. It remained the capital throughout the Sui and Tang dynasties. It was designed to be roughly square-shaped, with straight roads running north, south, east, and west, dividing the city into different areas. The biggest street was 1,345 feet wide! There were also royal gardens and a **polo** ground. There was an eastern market where more than 200 different types of Chinese businesses thrived and a western market for foreign traders and craftworkers, such as silversmiths.

After the fall of the Han empire, China was split up into many small kingdoms. In 581 General Yang Jian (541–604) set up the Sui dynasty (581–618) and reunited China by defeating his opponents. In 618 another general of the Sui court, Li Yan (566–635), joined a rebellion to overthrow the Sui ruler and established the Tang dynasty (618–906). The Tang dynasty ruled during the Golden Age of Chinese history. During the next 100 years of stability, agriculture and the textile industry advanced rapidly and the population of China increased. The granary in Luoyang could store 800 million pounds of grain—about half the total grain reserves of the state. The arts flourished and poetry in particular became popular throughout the country. Today we know of more than 10,000 poets from this period.

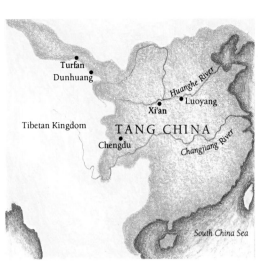

This is a map of the Tang empire showing Xi'an at its center.

This picture illustrates the Tang emperor Xuanzong watching his favorite concubine, Yang Guifei, trying to get on a horse.

The Capital City

During the Tang dynasty, the capital Xi'an was one of the largest cities in the world. Merchants came from all over the world to buy and sell goods. There was also an early banking system that allowed traders to deposit, and sometimes borrow, money. Xi'an was a truly international city with Korean, Japanese, Burmese, Arab, Persian, and African residents. These people were not only traders, but also scholars, monks, musicians, dancers, and athletes. Many aspects of foreign life became popular in Xi'an, such as the Persian game of polo, which was played by Tang aristocrats. The Tang emperor Xuanzong (685–762) even held international polo matches in his pleasure gardens and was a member of the Chinese polo team.

Princess Wencheng's Marriage

Chinese emperors usually tried to marry their daughters into the royal families of neighboring states. Their aim was to maintain good relations with their neighbors to protect the borders of their land. In 640, Songzan Ganbu (617–650), the king of Tibet, made a marriage proposal to the emperor of China's daughter, the Princess Wencheng. A year later the princess married the king. When Wencheng went to Tibet, she took some of the most up-to-date Chinese agricultural and weaving methods, some craftworkers, and the Chinese calendar. Songzan Ganbu built a castle and a palace for Wencheng and she lived in luxury in Lhasa, the capital.

The First Empress

Wu Zetian was born in 624. Her father was a merchant who later became an official, but he died when she was only 9 years old. At the age of 14 she was selected to be an **imperial concubine** and later she became the wife of Emperor Gaozong. In 690 he died and she became the first empress in Chinese history. During her reign she changed the examination system for selecting officials for central and local government so that people from poor backgrounds would have a chance to become officials. The Empress Wu was a Buddhist and built many temples and **pagodas**. Wu Zetian died in 705.

The First Empress, Wu Zetian

Traveling Monks and Famous Poetry

After 17 years, Xuanzang returned to the Tang capital, Xi'an, from India. He was welcomed by the emperor and people lined the road to catch a glimpse of him. His boxes of Buddhist books followed behind him on horses.

The journey from China to India was long and difficult. This ninth-century drawing shows a traveling monk with all his luggage on the road to India.

From the fourth to the eighth centuries, Buddhism became more popular than ever and many Buddhist monks longed to go to India to visit the birthplace of the Buddha.

Traveling Monks

The first recorded pilgrimage to India was made by the monk Faxian (sometimes called Fa Hsien), who left Xi'an in 399. When he arrived at Khotan, near the Chinese border, Faxian was impressed by the popularity of Buddhism there. He crossed the Pamir Mountains and visited many temples and shrines in Afghanistan and northern India. Twelve years later he returned home by sea.

Another traveling monk was Xuanzang (602–664). In some ways, Xuanzang's journey was even more difficult than Faxian's because the early Tang emperors did not allow people to travel abroad. Despite this, Xuanzang left Xi'an in 627 to travel to India. After traveling through Xinjiang, Afghanistan, Pakistan, India, Bangladesh, and Sri Lanka, he returned to Xi'an in 645 with hundreds of

volumes of Buddhist texts written in **Sanskrit**. The Tang emperor Taizong offered him financial support so that the Buddhist books could be translated into Chinese.

Many Buddhist books have been translated into Chinese. This is part of the ninth-century Lotus Sutra, which was brought to London, by Aurel Stein, from Dunhuang.

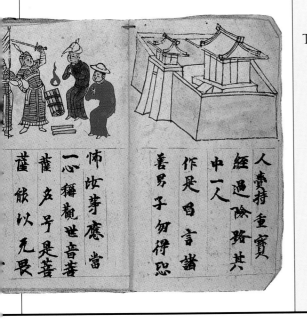

Famous Poetry

During the Tang period every educated person could write both poetry and prose. Poetry even became an important part of the examination to get a job in local government! The most famous Tang poets are Li Bo (701–762) and Du Fu (712–770), whose poems are still popular in China today.

Li Bo

Li Bo was born in Chinese Central Asia in 701. As a young man he traveled a great deal and wrote poems wherever he went. Li Bo was so famous that Emperor Xuanzong invited him to join the court at Xi'an, but Li Bo did not get on well with the officials there and left. It is said that he drowned in a river trying to catch the reflection of the moon in the water.

Li Bo

Du Fu

Du Fu is famous as a poet of Chinese history. He was born into an official's family and passed the examinations to become an official himself. Du Fu was a good friend of Li Bo's and they traveled together through Henan and Shandong. While Li Bo's poems are very playful and entertaining, Du Fu's poems reflect the more serious side of life and society.

Du Fu

Two Poems

The first poem is by Li Bo and the second by Du Fu.

My native country, untroubled times are always in my thoughts.
My friend is lodging in the Eastern mountains,
Dearly loving the beauty of valleys and hills,
At green spring he lies in the empty woods,
And is still asleep when the sun shines on high.

Well said, Chang'an looks like a chessboard –
Won and lost for a hundred years, sad beyond all telling.
The mansions of princes and nobles all have new lords,
And another generation wears the caps and robes of office.
Due north in the mountain passes the gongs and drums shake.
To the chariots and horses campaigning in the west the winged
  dispatches hasten.
While the fish and dragons fall asleep and the autumn river
  turns cold.

4 China after the Tenth Century

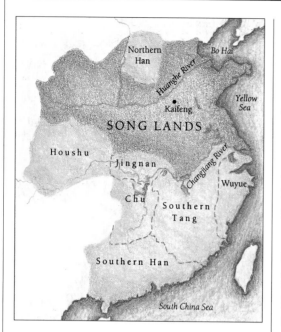

The purple area shows the center of the Song dynasty. The orange area shows the states that were brought under Song control.

Trade and Cities

Another peasant rebellion at the end of the ninth century led to the downfall of the Tang dynasty and once again China was divided into different kingdoms. In 960 General Zhao Kuangyin (927–976) snatched the throne from the emperor, who was only seven years old. He named his new dynasty the Song dynasty (960–1279), and made Kaifeng his capital city.

Mining, textiles, papermaking, and printing all developed very quickly during the Song dynasty. The porcelain industry was particularly important. Though porcelain had been exported to Japan, Korea, south Asia, and Africa during the Tang dynasty, improvements in shipping, such as the invention of the compass (see box on page 31), meant that more porcelain could be traded overseas.

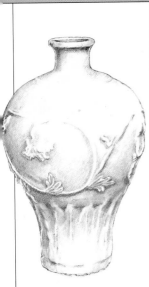

An example of Song porcelain

This *famous scroll (rolled) painting measures over 16 feet when it is unrolled and is called* Spring Festival on the River.

A Wealthy City

Kaifeng was blessed with natural advantages. It was surrounded by a natural moat, and trade flourished in the city because of its position in the middle of China. There were hundreds of 24-hour restaurants, and many markets and theaters entertained the thousands of merchants passing through. All types of theater were popular, and performances of opera, puppetry, and acrobatics were held in massive theaters—the largest theater could hold more than 1,000 people. Festivals were held every week in the famous Xiangguo Temple, where people came to buy and sell clothes, books, furniture, and pets.

Paper Money

The Chinese invented paper money during the Song period. Paper money had two main advantages over money made out of silver, gold, copper, or iron: It was easier to carry around and the copper and iron could be saved for use in everyday objects. Names and **seals** were printed and written on paper money by the government officials who issued it. When Marco Polo (see pages 28–29) traveled to China in the 13th century, he was so impressed by paper money that he described how it was made, used, and valued. Paper money was not used in Europe until the 17th century.

A *square was cut in the middle of Chinese coins so that merchants could carry them around on strings. The "coins" above are actually money charms.*

S*ilver was one of the important currencies in China. This picture shows a silversmith cutting ingots (blocks).*

T*he lion dance is performed during the Chinese New Year celebrations. It is usually performed by two or three people.*

The Arts and Sciences

Scholars and artists were highly respected at the Song court. In this picture Emperor Huizong is entertaining his guests.

Most Chinese books were printed with this type of woodblock.

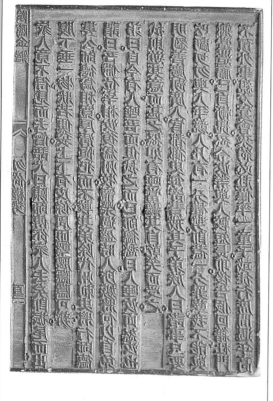

Many outstanding scientific discoveries were made during the Song period. Sheng Kuo (1031–1095) wrote a famous book, *Dream Stream Essays,* which explored **astronomy**, chemistry, mathematics, geology, **physics**, architecture, and medicine. This book tells us about many inventors and their creations.

Printing

Before printing was invented, every book had to be copied by hand. In the seventh century, the Chinese invented wood-block printing. The text was first written on a piece of thin paper, then glued face down onto a wooden plate. The characters (letters or words) were carved out to make a wood-block printing plate, which was used to print the text. Wood-block printing took a long time as a new block had to be carved for every page in a book.

Bi Sheng (died c. 1051) invented movable type printing around 1041 to 1048. He made a separate block for each character out of clay, so that they could be arranged into a block for printing and then later reused. This invention was as revolutionary in its time as the computer has been in the 20th century. Books could be printed more easily and faster than ever before. For example, in 1298, 100 copies of a 60,000-word book were printed in less than a month.

Calligraphy and Painting

During the Song period, officials and rich merchants enjoyed all the arts, but especially **calligraphy** and painting. The Song emperor Huizong (1082–1135) was an artist and kept a painting school at his court. Artists who passed the school's exams could become professional painters.

Porcelain

The Song period was the Classical Age of the porcelain industry. Song porcelain is renowned for its beauty and also for the way it was made. For example, the Longquan kiln in Zhejiang Province could fire (bake) 20,000 to 25,000 pots at once. In the 11th century, the art of porcelain making found its way to central Asia. Europeans didn't start to make porcelain until the 15th century.

Gunpowder

Gunpowder is a mixture of **saltpeter**, **sulfur**, and charcoal. In the tenth century, weapon-makers in China discovered that if they combined gunpowder and arrows they could create a new weapon. This new explosive crossbow destroyed their enemies. Forty thousand workers produced several thousand of these weapons every day in the Song capital. In the middle of the 13th century, the Arabs learned how to make gunpowder from the Chinese and called it "China snow". Europeans eventually found out about gunpowder from the Arabs.

*T*his picture shows two Chinese soldiers using crossbows.

Medicine

Chinese doctors use herbal medicine and acupuncture to cure their patients. When they treat patients with acupuncture, they place needles at various points on the body to cure illness. For example, needles in the hand sometimes help to relieve headaches.

In 1026, Wang Weiyi, a doctor in the royal hospital, designed two bronze statuettes showing all the acupuncture needle points on the human body. This type of model is still used for teaching medical students today.

Li Shizhen (1518-1593) wrote his magnificent book, *Compendium of Materia Medica,* in the 16th century. It illustrates nearly 2,000 herbs and lists 11,000 remedies.

Astronomy

As early as the second century A.D., Zhang Heng (78–139) built a **celestial globe**. In 1088, Han Gonglian designed the first water-driven astronomical clock in the world. It took three years to build, was 39 feet tall, and had nearly 200 wooden puppets in its five levels that beat drums and made beautiful sounds.

*T*he science of astronomy was very advanced in China. This is an 18th-century drawing of the royal observatory.

5 New Travelers

The Mongols and the Arrival of Foreigners

An illustrated manuscript showing the fierceness of the Mongol cavalry

The Mongols were a tribe of nomads who lived on the Mongolian grasslands, or steppes. In the 13th century Genghis Khan (c. 1167–1227) united all the nomads of the steppes (about six large tribes) by defeating them all in battle, and in doing so established the Mongol empire. When Genghis Khan died, his grandson Kublai Khan (1260–1294) led the Mongolian army into battle against the Song dynasty and defeated it. In 1271, he moved his government to Peking (called Yanjing at the time) and established the Yuan dynasty. During the 13th century, the Mongols took control of large areas of China and central Asia and even attacked Europe.

The Mongols had various contacts outside China, in particular with the **Muslims** from central and western Asia, and they employed many foreigners in their government. More Europeans began to find their way to China and these explorers brought many Chinese inventions back to the West.

There are plenty of stories about the Europeans who traveled to, or wanted to travel to, China during this time. Friar William's expedition (see page 27) was unsuccessful but Marco Polo's journey (see pages 28–29) was a success.

Yuan Drama

The Mongols took great pleasure in drama. As it was difficult for Chinese people to get an official post in the Mongolian government, many Chinese writers devoted their time and talents to writing plays for the theater instead. Guan Hanqing (c. 1220–1300) was the most famous playwright of this time. He wrote more than 60 plays, and some of them are still enjoyed by people today. Ji Junxiang was another Yuan playwright. His work *Chinese Orphan* was performed in Paris in August 1755.

In this scene from a Yuan play, the girl is playing a musical instrument called a piba.

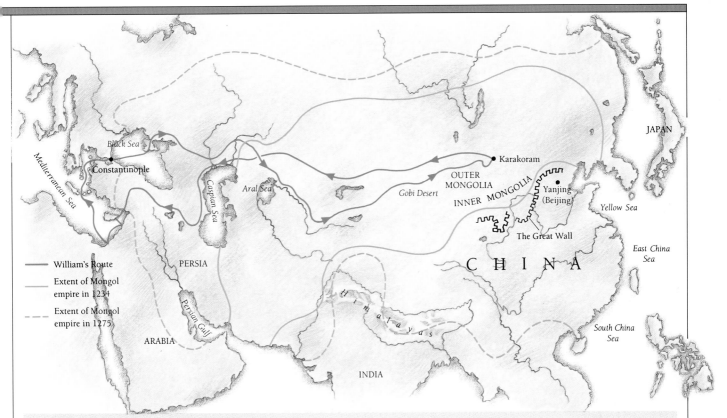

A *Mongol woman and her children in front of their yurt home (above). The grasslands of Mongolia (below and background) are home to 20 million people.*

Friar William

Friar William was a priest at the court of the French king Louis IX. In 1253 he decided to travel to the East to bring Christianity to the Mongols. He set off from Constantinople (modern-day Istanbul in Turkey) and made his way toward the Black Sea (see map). After traveling for a month by boat and on horseback he met the Mongols and stayed with them for several months before finally reaching Karakoram. The Mongols thought that Friar William was a spy and wouldn't let him travel freely. Friar William wrote about the people he met and the places he visited. He described Mongolian yurts, or houses: "They set up the dwelling in which they sleep on a circular frame of interlaced sticks converging into a little round hoop on the top." Unfortunately, Friar William never crossed the Great Wall and did not reach China, but he probably met some Chinese people because he mentioned the Song dynasty (see pages 22–23), Chinese paper money, and Chinese writing.

The Story of Marco Polo

Marco Polo (1254–1324) was born in Venice. Marco's father, Nicolas, and uncle, Maffeo, were merchants who traveled to central Asia to do business in 1260. At Bokhara they met some Chinese **envoys** who invited them to China. They arrived in China in 1265, stayed for about a year, and met Kublai Khan. They returned to Venice in 1269, but left again for China in 1271. This time Marco went with them and didn't return to Venice until 1295, 24 years after he had set out on his adventure.

A Difficult Journey

The Polos journeyed toward the Persian Gulf, passed through the city of Baghdad, and sailed up the Tigris River before walking across western Turkestan, through Balkh and the Pamir Mountains. Their journey was very dangerous as they had to overcome all the difficulties of crossing high, cold mountains and hot, waterless deserts. Finally, four years after they had left Venice, they met Kublai Khan at Shangtu, the Mongolian capital. Marco Polo stayed in China for 17 years, traveling all over the country and writing about everything he saw and did.

Marco Polo in Peking

Marco was impressed by the city of Peking (modern-day Beijing). He described the palace, streets, and markets where he saw paper money for the first time. The walled city had 12 gates, which was more than any European city of the time. The streets were very wide and ran straight across the city. Merchants brought precious stones, pearls, spices, and many more things from all over the world to sell in the markets.

A picture of Marco Polo and his father and uncle from a Spanish map

Markets and Banquets

In his famous book, *The Travels of Marco Polo*, Marco wrote about the markets of Peking: "No fewer than a thousand packhorses and carriages, loaded with raw silk from the Chinese provinces, make their daily entry." He also described banquets held in the royal palace. The banquet hall was large enough to seat 6,000 guests, and the tables were decorated with carved animals and bowls and cups of silver and gold. At important banquets an orchestra played, singers and dancers performed, and elephants and lions were put on show.

Marco Polo and his father and uncle leaving Venice for China

Marco Polo also visited Suzhou, which is near Hangzhou.

Marco Polo in Hangzhou

Kublai Khan appointed Marco Polo as an official of the **Privy Council** in 1277 and for three years he was a tax inspector in Yangzhou. He frequently visited Hangzhou, another city very near Yangzhou. At one time Hangzhou was the capital of the Song dynasty (see pages 22–23) and had a beautiful lake and many canals, rather like Marco's hometown of Venice. Marco fell in love with it and wrote, "There are said to be 12,000 bridges, mostly of stone, though some are of wood. Those over the main channels and the chief thoroughfare are built with lofty arches and are so well designed that big ships without a mast can pass under them, and yet carts and horses also pass over them, so well is the street level adjusted to the height."

This map shows the journeys of Marco Polo. Marco, his father, and his uncle traveled to many places before they reached China.

Ibn Battuta

Ibn Battuta (1304–1368) was a great Arab traveler who visited China in the 14th century. Arab and Iranian traders were the main contacts between China and Europe during the 14th century and sea trading developed rapidly. Muslims went to Southeast Asia and China to do business, and a number of them lived in cities on the southeast coast of China, particularly in Quanzhou and Canton (modern-day Guangzhou).

Ibn Battuta was born into a judge's family in Morocco and started his long journey through Africa and Asia when he was only 21. In India Ibn Battuta met some Chinese ambassadors and decided to go to China with them. In April 1346 they set sail from Samudra and reached the coast of China about four months later, after passing through the Maldive Islands, Sri Lanka, and Java. Ibn Battuta announced to Chinese officials that he was the ambassador of the Muslim ruler of India and the Chinese emperor invited him to the capital. On his way to Peking (modern-day Beijing) he visited the city of Hangzhou and was welcomed with banquets, plays, and canal trips. Like Marco Polo, Ibn Battuta was impressed by Chinese paper money, which was still unknown in the West.

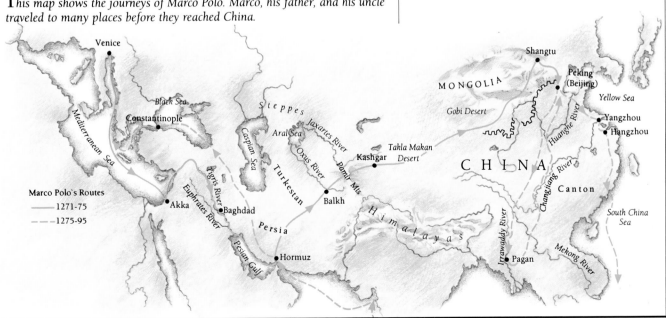

29

Zheng He's Journeys

In the middle of the 14th century the Chinese people overthrew the Mongol Yuan dynasty, and restored their own rule in China. This period became known as the Ming dynasty (1368–1644). The new emperor was Zhu Yuanzhang. He was also known as the Beggar King, because he had spent some years as a traveling monk before his successful rebellion against the Mongols. The new Ming capital was Peking and it took 13 years to build the royal palace.

During the Ming dynasty, China's relations with other countries underwent a number of changes. In the north, great attention was paid to rebuilding the Great Wall to keep out the nomad invaders of the steppes. The Ming emperors did not allow ordinary people to travel to foreign lands, but they did let their officials travel abroad in order to increase their political influence, particularly in Southeast Asia.

Zheng He's story was described in 17th-century popular fiction. This picture is taken from one of these popular books. The soldier is holding a banner that calls Zheng He "The Great Commander of the Ming."

An artist's impression of ships from Zheng He's fleet

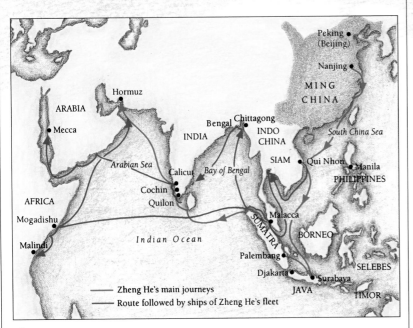

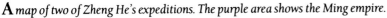

A *map of two of Zheng He's expeditions. The purple area shows the Ming empire.*

Zheng He's Treasure Ships

Zheng He (1371–1435) is the most famous sea traveler of Chinese history. He came from a Muslim family in Yunnan and was sent to the royal household to be a **eunuch** and serve the emperor when he was a child. At the imperial court, he became a Buddhist and is known as the Grand Buddhist Eunuch.

Between 1405 and 1433, the emperor Cheng Zu sent Zheng He on seven voyages of discovery overseas, reaching as far as Southeast Asia, India, the Persian Gulf, and East Africa. Zheng He's treasure ships carried enormous quantities of gifts from the emperor, which he presented everywhere he went. On one of his expeditions his 62 ships carried a total of 28,000 men. Each ship weighed 15,000 tons. It was the largest fleet in the world at that time.

Shipbuilding

Chinese shipbuilding started in the seventh century B.C. and was the most advanced in the world by the 13th and 14th centuries A.D.. The most famous Chinese ship was called the sand ship. It had a flat bottom that could take loads of 500 to 800 tons. Chinese shipyards made thousands of ships every year, and these were used by Arabian, Asian, and African traders as well as the Chinese.

A *illustration of one of the earliest compasses. The lodestone (a magnetic iron stone that always points north) floats in water in the center of the bronze compass.*

The Compass

Without a compass, Zheng He's journeys across the Pacific Ocean would not have been possible. The compass was invented in China more than 2,000 years ago. The compass was taken to the Middle East and then to Europe in the 12th century. It was used in all voyages of exploration. Columbus's discovery of the Americas (1492) and Magellan's around-the-world voyage (1519–1521) relied on the compass.

Xu Xiake: An Unusual Traveler

Xu Xiake (1586–1641) was one of the greatest Chinese travelers and explorers. He was born in Jiangyin in the province of Jiangsu. When he was very young, he became interested in travel and geography, but because he took care of his old mother he could not go away for long periods of time.

A *portrait of Xu Xiake. His book is still read by many people today.*

A Dangerous Journey

After Xu Xiake's mother died, he traveled to the remotest areas of south China, where no one had gone before. In September 1636, he left Jiangyin and headed to Zhejiang with a fellow monk, Jingwen. Unfortunately, Jingwen was murdered by some bandits and Xu carried his ashes to the famous Chicken Feet Mountain in Yunnan and buried him in sacred Buddhist land. Xu continued his journey, but the roads were very difficult to travel along, and sometimes there wasn't a road at all. Xu traveled through the provinces of Jiangxi, Hunan, Guangxi, and Guizhou and reached Tengchong in Yunnan in April 1639. After narrowly escaping a fall from the top of a cliff on his way into the city, Xu discovered that he had lost all his money and had to sell his clothes to buy food.

Flowers and Butterflies

Xu Xiake wrote about the huge camellias (a type of flower) he saw in Yunnan. Xu wrote about fabulous flowers again when he visited the famous Taihua Temple in the provincial capital of Kunming. In Dali, Xu visited the Butterfly Pool, a place where thousands of butterflies come to rest on a tree by a pool. You can still visit these places today as a modern explorer.

Xu wanted to go on to Burma (modern-day Myanmar) but could not find a guide to take him there. On his journey home he fell ill and died a few months later at the age of 56.

A painting on silk of a group of travelers making their way through some of the high mountains of China. The painting dates from the Tang dynasty (see pages 18–22). Xu Xiake would also have traveled through scenery like this on horseback.

The Three White Pagodas in Dali, Yunnan, built during the Tang period. Xu Xiake described this place in his book.

There are many high mountains in Yunnan that Xu Xiake made detailed notes about in his book.

Two sisters from the mountains of Yunnan

6 Europe and China

The Conflict between Two Different Worlds

A *map of European trade routes*

In the 15th century, the **Turks** took control of the overland silk and spice route between China and the West. The Europeans were furious about this and sent their sailors to find alternative sea routes to the East so that they could trade with a greater number of people through a greater number of routes. At the same time the Roman Catholic Church wanted to increase its influence in the East and sent **missionaries** to China.

A Jesuit Priest

Matteo Ricci (1552–1609) was born in Macerata in Italy. He studied in the **Jesuit** school in his hometown and then went to Rome to study law. In Rome he became interested in the East (also known at this time as the Orient). In 1582, Ricci arrived in Macao as a missionary. Ricci learned Chinese, befriended many high-ranking Chinese officials, and converted some of them to Christianity. He was invited by Emperor Wanli to the Forbidden City (see box on page 38) but failed to convert him to Christianity.

Ricci introduced many aspects of European culture such as **cartography** and mathematics to China. When Ricci died, he was buried in Peking (modern-day Beijing).

A Tourist at the Great Wall

Johann Grueber (1623–1680) was a German Jesuit priest who set out from Venice for China in 1656. After reaching Peking, he stayed in China for three years and worked as a missionary (along with 56 other Jesuits) baptizing Chinese converts to Christianity.

Grueber left Peking in June 1661 with the French Jesuit monk Albert d'Orville and traveled for 60 days before arriving at Xining, a city near the Great Wall. Grueber described the distance between two of the gates on the wall as being a walk of 18 days. Grueber was also impressed by the width of the wall, saying that it was so wide that "six horsemen may run abreast on it without embarrassing each other."

After leaving Xining, Grueber and d'Orville traveled on to Lhasa in Tibet and were probably the first Europeans to enter the city.

Matteo Ricci is seen here with his Chinese friend Xu Guanqi, a Ming official. Ricci is dressed in traditional Chinese clothes.

The Qing Empire

In 1644, the Ming government was overthrown by a series of peasant rebellions. The **Manchus** of the Mongolian grasslands then defeated the peasant armies and established their own dynasty, called the Qing dynasty (1644–1911). Like the Mongols, the Manchus were very good soldiers and used their skills to expand the Qing empire.

By the eighteenth century, Britain was the leading **industrial** power in the West and was keen to trade with China. In 1792, Lord George Macartney (1737–1806) took a delegation of 135 people to China to meet the emperor.

They set sail from Portsmouth in September and arrived in China the following year. Macartney took several artists with him and they recorded the things they saw in beautiful watercolors, which they took back to Britain. Macartney took Emperor Qianlong presents as tokens of his goodwill but still failed in his mission to open up more British trade with China. One of the reasons for this failure was Macartney's refusal to kneel down at the feet of the emperor, called kowtowing. The kowtow was a traditional way of showing respect to the emperor.

Emperor Qianlong employed a number of foreigners as court artists. This picture was painted by an Italian named Giuseppe Castiglione (1688–1766).

William Alexander (1767–1816), one of the artists who went to China with Lord Macartney, made this drawing of the Western Gate of Peking.

The First Opium War

In 1839, the First Opium War broke out between China and Britain over the trade in the drug **opium**. The English East India Company sold opium taken from British India to China in order to pay for Chinese imports such as tea, silk, and porcelain. People in China gradually became more and more addicted to opium and spent vast sums of money on the drug. The Chinese government became worried as its treasury was being drained. In 1839 the Chinese government seized more than 20,000 chests of Indian opium in protest and burned them in Canton. The British retaliated by sending 4,000 troops to attack major Chinese ports and cities. The British eventually won the war and a treaty was signed in Nanjing in August 1842, which gave The British the right to trade in China. The island of Hong Kong was handed over as part of the peace treaty.

The Second Opium War

On October 8, 1856, Chinese officials arrested Chinese sailors belonging to a British ship in Canton harbor. The British were offended by Chinese interference in their business affairs and demanded an apology. The Chinese

The Taiping Rebellion

It was not only Westerners who caused trouble in China. In 1851, Hong Xiuquan (1814–1864) led a rebellion from the southwest of China and set up his own kingdom, which he called the Heavenly Kingdom of Great Peace, in Nanjing. Hong came from a farming background and was inspired by Christian teachings. He dreamed that he was the younger brother of Jesus Christ and that it was his mission to save China. His revolution lasted for 13 years and affected half of China.

Chinese ships fighting the British navy during the First Opium War. The Chinese lost the Opium War and were forced to open their ports to foreigners.

The Summer Palace was destroyed by British and French troops in 1856.

government refused to apologize and crowds of protesters burned British shops and factories in Canton. This is how another trading war, called the Second Opium War (even though it had nothing to do with opium), began. Anglo-French troops occupied Peking and set fire to the Imperial Summer Palace. The Summer Palace was one of the finest buildings in the world, built in both Chinese and European styles of architecture. It contained many precious treasures and a royal library. Before destroying the Summer Palace, the British and French troops grabbed as much as they could carry away with them. A British soldier wrote "You can scarcely imagine the beauty and magnificence of the buildings we burnt. It made one's heart sore to burn them... It was wretchedly demoralizing work for an army. Everybody was wild for plunder." Now only a few ruins of the palace are left.

By the early 19th century there were plenty of foreigners living in China. This European painting shows different flags hung on ships and buildings.

Scientist Explorers

When China opened its doors to foreigners in the 19th century, many Western scientists arrived to study the country's animals and plants. In 1803, William Kerr was sent to China by the Royal Gardens at Kew (London) to collect plants from the Far East. Another famous plant collector was Robert Fortune, who studied at the Royal Botanic Gardens in Edinburgh. In 1843 Fortune was appointed by the Royal Horticultural Society at Chiswick in London as their special plant collector in China. Fortune traveled all over China for nine years and found many new plants.

Between 1864 and 1874 the Frenchman Père Jean Pierre David (1826–1900), made three journeys into China, traveling from Peking to Mongolia and from Tibet to Sichuan by boat, horse, and on foot. Père David was probably the first Westerner to discover the giant panda in March 1869 while traveling between the borders of Tibet and Sichuan. Some local hunters killed a white "bear" and sent it to him. Père David wrote in his diary, "Is it possible that it is new to science?" and sent the skin and skull of the panda back to Paris, where it was identified as a species that was new to the West.

The Last Emperor

The Child Emperor

Pu Yi was born in 1906 when the Qing dynasty was coming to its end. Emperor Guangxu's wife, Ci Xi, imprisoned the emperor and made herself the head of state. Guangxu died in November 1908 and Ci Xi (called the Empress Dowager) chose two-year-old Pu Yi as the new emperor of China. She knew he was too young to rule, which meant that she would have more power. But the empress died just a few months later. When Pu Yi was five years old, China became a republic (a country with an elected government rather than one ruled by a king or queen), but the new government allowed him to carry on living in the Forbidden City. Pu Yi learned to read and write with his servants and practiced calligraphy for hours every day. Pu Yi had a British tutor, Reginald Johnston, who visited the palace almost every day from March 1919 until 1922.

Empress Ci Xi and the child emperor Pu Yi

The Forbidden City

Peking (modern-day Beijing) was the old capital of the Yuan dynasty (see page 26). In 1421, Emperor Cheng Zu, of the Ming dynasty, decided to move his capital to Peking and turned the Forbidden City into the Imperial Palace. The Forbidden City occupies 864,000 square yards, took 15 years to build, and is right in the middle of Peking. It has nearly 100,000 rooms and is surrounded by a moat. The city is divided into two sections: One area is made up of large ceremonial halls for conducting official business and the other contains living quarters and gardens. The front entrance of the palace is called the Gate of Heavenly Peace.

*L*ike all Chinese emperors, Pu Yi had many wives. This photo is of Pu Yi and his favorite wife, Wan Rong, in Tianjin, together with their foreign friends.

During the 1930s, the Japanese expanded their empire and marched into China. Pu Yi was persuaded to go to Manchuria (where he originally came from) by the Japanese to act as the emperor during their occupation. Pu Yi's life was controlled by the Japanese, and the Russian army arrested him when the Japanese left China after World War II (1939–1945). After some time in prison the last emperor of China later worked as a gardener in Peking (modern-day Beijing) and died in 1967 at the beginning of the Cultural Revolution (see pages 43–44).

The First Railroad in China

The first railroad in China was built in Shanghai in 1874 with money raised by British companies. People came from miles around to see trains for the first time. Often a wall of people would stand along the side of the tracks watching the trains. Tickets were very expensive: The price of a first-class ticket from Shanghai to Wusong was the same amount as rice for a family for one month. However, the railroad was built without a proper license and the Chinese government had it dismantled.

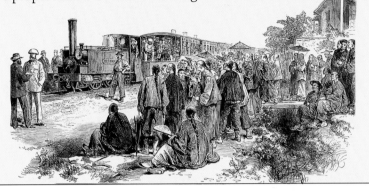

Shanghai: An Adventurer's Paradise

Seven hundred years ago, Shanghai was a small fishing village. It became larger during the Yuan (see page 26) and Ming (see page 30) dynasties, but was often under attack from Japanese pirates. In 1832, the first British boat to China arrived at the port of Wusong, but was fired upon by the Chinese army. The peace settlement of the First Opium War made Shanghai one of the five open ports where Westerners were allowed to trade. More and more foreigners went to Shanghai to do business and hundreds of foreign shops, banks, clubs, and restaurants sprang up. Most foreign visitors lived in special districts rented from the government.

*T*he port of Shanghai during the 1930s

7 Modern China

Revolution and Change

The New Culture

On May 4, 1919, about 3,000 students organized a demonstration in Peking to protest against the Treaty of Versailles, the peace treaty signed by the allies after World War I (1914–1918). The treaty gave Japan control over northeast China and the students objected to this. This demonstration was important because it marked the beginning of the "New Culture"—new ways of scientific and political thinking.

On October 10, 1911, a revolution transformed China from an imperial empire into a republic, when the Manchu Emperor was overthrown. The first president of China was Sun Yat-Sen (1866–1925), who ruled at the head of his **Nationalist** Party.

The Nationalists and the Communists

In 1912, a group of Nationalists, led by Sun Yat-Sen, formed their own party called the Kuomintang, or KMT. This was the beginning of the Nationalist Revolution.

In 1921, a group of people in Shanghai were influenced by the writings of **Karl Marx** and set up the Communist Party. After the death of Sun Yat-Sen in 1925, General Chiang Kai-Shek took over the leadership of the Nationalists. In Canton in 1926, Chiang Kai-Shek led the Nationalist army, which joined with the Communists to fight the warlords (powerful landowners) in the north and unite the nation. Once the warlords had been defeated, the Nationalists hunted out Communists, threw them out of their party, and killed anyone who opposed them. The Communists fled to Jiangxi, hid in the mountains, and gradually rebuilt their power. In 1934 the Nationalists forced the Communists to retreat again. To escape attack, the Communists began the Long March.

A *Nationalist soldier (left) and a Communist guerrilla (below). The Communist army consisted mostly of poor peasants.*

After more than a year of the Long March, the Red Army reached Yan'an. This is a photograph of Chairman Mao and General Zhu Te with an American journalist and an unknown woman in 1937.

Mao liked to give speeches to his soldiers and to ordinary people, but because his accent was so strong people did not find him easy to understand.

The Long March

Late in 1934, the Red Army of about 100,000 people left Jiangxi to travel to Yan'an. They marched through many provinces, climbed over 18 mountain ranges, crossed 24 rivers, and trekked through marshes, deserts, and snow-covered mountains with only thin cotton clothes to keep them warm. Only one in every five people who set out on the march survived. The people who lived through the march walked almost 6,000 miles in a year. The Communists made Yan'an their headquarters from 1936 to 1945 and conducted **guerrilla** warfare and educational and agricultural reform programs from this base.

The leader of the Long March was Mao Zedong (1893–1976), a former teacher who became one of the founding members of the Chinese Communist Party. Mao was the son of a farmer and it was to the country that he returned to find support for his ideas.

41

Chairman Mao wanted everyone in China to become soldiers so everyone had to undergo military training.

This is a photograph of Chairman Mao addressing a massive crowd of his supporters in Beijing in the 1970s.

Chairman Mao Rules China

By 1937 the Nationalist government was losing support because it had failed to stop the Japanese invading China (see page 39). The Communists in Yan'an were fighting the Japanese more successfully through their guerrilla tactics and people became aware of this. China was plunged into a civil war between the Nationalists and the Communists in 1946 after the Japanese had been defeated in World War II. After nearly three years of fighting, on October 1, 1949, Mao Zedong stood at the Gate of Heavenly Peace in front of the Forbidden City (see page 38) and proclaimed the establishment of the People's Republic of China. The Nationalist government fled to Taiwan, an island off the coast of China in the Pacific Ocean.

The Cultural Revolution was a mass demonstration of the people's power. Thousands of people went on marches, holding Chairman Mao's portrait and shouting slogans.

The Cultural Revolution

The Communist government tried to create a new society. In the first years of Communist power many reforms were brought in dividing land equally among the people and forbidding **arranged marriages**. But there were also negative sides to Communist rule. In 1958, Mao announced the Great Leap Forward—a campaign to encourage opponents of the Communists to speak out. With Mao's encouragement, many intellectuals voiced their opinions and were then killed or sent to work in forced labor camps.

In the ten years from 1966 to 1976, Chairman Mao's **Red Guards** tried to destroy traditional customs, books, and clothes. This movement was called the Cultural Revolution. It was a disastrous experiment. People who had foreign connections were persecuted, and musicians, dancers, surgeons, and university professors were exiled to the borders of China where they were forced to do hard labor. Thousands of people died and China's door was firmly shut to the West. When Chairman Mao died on September 9, 1976, at the age of 83, the Cultural Revolution died with him and was renamed the Ten Years of Chaos.

American Zoologists Explore

In 1916, three **zoologists** from the American Museum of Natural History set out with a Chinese interpreter and five Chinese assistants to explore the natural history of Yunnan Province. At this time Yunnan was one of the most inaccessible places in China because of its high mountains and ethnic groups who were often at war with one another.

The yearlong expedition collected many specimens from the peoples of the province, as an entry from the expedition's diary shows: "We let it be known that we would pay well for specimens, and there was an almost uninterrupted procession of men and boys carrying long sticks, on which were strung frogs, rats, toads and snakes. They would simply beam with triumph and enthusiasm. Our fame spread and more came, bringing the most ridiculous tame things—pigeons, Maltese cats, dogs, white rabbits, caged birds. ..."

Even children joined the Cultural Revolution. They were called the Little Red Guards.

China Today

In the late 1970s, China adopted the "open door policy" because it was eager to take an active part in international affairs again. Factory owners were given more power, workers were paid to produce more, and in 1977 there was a nationwide pay increase. The new government also allowed the return of markets, which had been banned during the Cultural Revolution. This allowed farmers to produce more varied types of food, make more money, and put an end to **rationing**, which had existed throughout the Cultural Revolution. Farmers were gradually allowed to work by themselves on their own land instead of in large **communes** on government land. When people worked in communes, everything they produced was given to the state so there was no **incentive** to produce more because no one was allowed to keep what they grew. With the re-introduction of private land, people had more reason to work hard as they could benefit from it directly.

Looking to the Future

Modern-day China's aim is to develop the economy and to modernize the country by the end of the 20th century. The Chinese government has set up special economic zones to encourage foreign companies to invest in new technology. China is also looking forward to 1997, when it takes over the wealthy island of Hong Kong from Britain.

Young Chinese people are growing up in a country very different from that of their parent's youth. Many young people can speak a foreign language such as English, French, or German and many Chinese students go abroad to study. There are also more foreigners working or studying in China. The youth of China is now growing up in a truly international world where there is more and more opportunity to discover and explore their own and other cultures.

Tiananmen Square

The square in front of the entrance to the Forbidden City, known as the Gate of Heavenly Peace, has always been at the center of Chinese political life. Ancient imperial governments gave orders in the square and the famous New Culture movement proclaimed itself from the square. After the Communist Revolution, Mao's government pulled down several buildings to make Tiananmen Square the largest of its kind in the world. Mass Communist marches have been held in this huge space and Chairman Mao's body is housed in a building behind it. Tiananmen Square has always been a famous tourist attraction and focus of international attention. On June 4, 1989, the square made the headlines once again. Students demonstrating for democracy and reform were massacred by troops in a shocking show of force by the Chinese government.

The student demonstration of 1989 in front of the Forbidden City

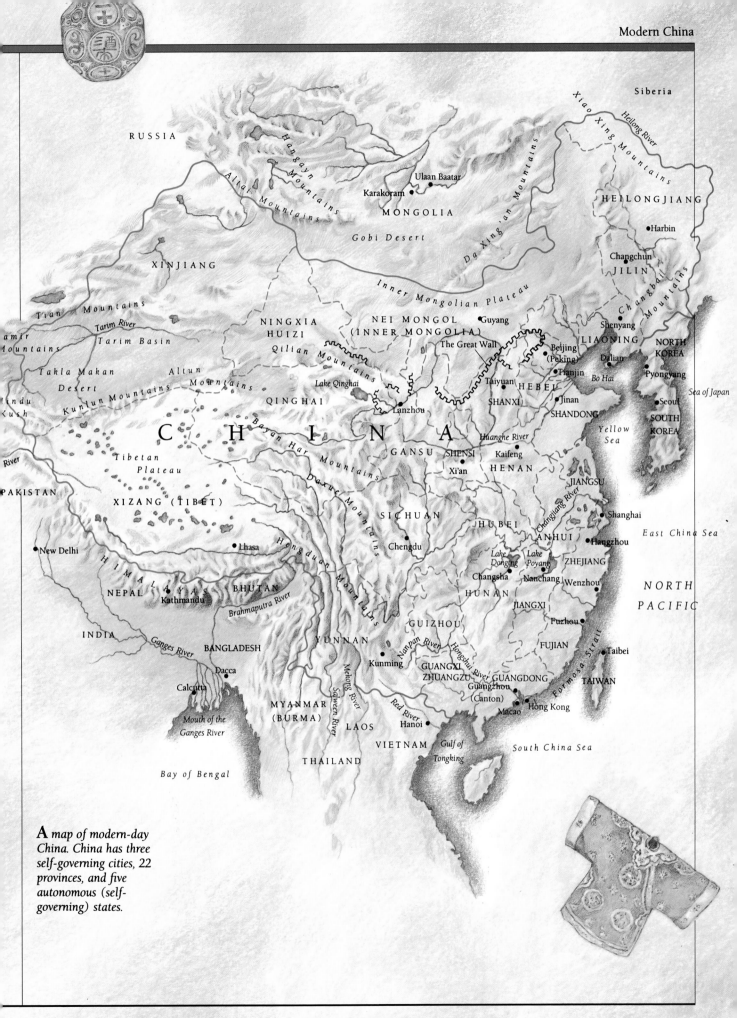

RUSSIA

Siberia

Altai Mountains

Hangayn Mountains

Xiao Xing Mountains

Heilong River

MONGOLIA

Karakoram
Ulaan Baatar

HEILONGJIANG

Gobi Desert

Harbin

Da Xing'an Mountains

Changchun

JILIN

XINJIANG

Inner Mongolian Plateau

Shenyang

Changbai Mountains

Tian Mountains

NINGXIA HUIZI

NEI MONGOL (INNER MONGOLIA)

Guyang

LIAONING

Dalian

NORTH KOREA

Pamir Mountains

Tarim River

Tarim Basin

Qilian Mountains

The Great Wall

Beijing (Peking)

Tianjin

Bo Hai

Pyongyang

Takla Makan Desert

Altun Mountains

Lake Qinghai

Taiyuan

HEBEI

Jinan

Yellow Sea

Sea of Japan

Hindu Kush

Kunlun Mountains

QINGHAI

Lanzhou

SHANXI

SHANDONG

Seoul

SOUTH KOREA

River

C   H   I   N   A

Bayan Har Mountains

Huanghe River

GANSU

SHENSI

Kaifeng

PAKISTAN

Tibetan Plateau

Daxue Mountains

Xi'an

HENAN

JIANGSU

New Delhi

XIZANG (TIBET)

Lhasa

Hengduan Mountains

SICHUAN

Chengdu

HUBEI

ANHUI

Changjiang River

Shanghai

East China Sea

Hangzhou

HIMALAYAS

Brahmaputra River

Lake Dongting

Lake Poyang

ZHEJIANG

NEPAL

BHUTAN

Kathmandu

Changsha

Nanchang

Wenzhou

NORTH PACIFIC

INDIA

Ganges River

BANGLADESH

HUNAN

JIANGXI

YUNNAN

GUIZHOU

Fuzhou

FUJIAN

Dacca

Calcutta

Mouth of the Ganges River

MYANMAR (BURMA)

Mekong River

Salween River

Nanpan River

Kunming

Hongshui River

GUANGXI ZHUANGZU

GUANGDONG

Guangzhou (Canton)

Formosa Strait

Taibei

TAIWAN

Macao

Hong Kong

LAOS

Red River

Hanoi

VIETNAM

Gulf of Tongking

South China Sea

THAILAND

Bay of Bengal

A map of modern-day China. China has three self-governing cities, 22 provinces, and five autonomous (self-governing) states.

China	Europe	Other
c. 6000–5000 B.C. Farming villages thrive along the Huanghe River Valley.	**c. 6500 B.C.** Farming begins in Greece and spreads to other areas of Europe.	**c. 5000 B.C.** Farming begins in western parts of India.
c. 1600–1100 The Shang dynasty. The Shang make bronzes and write on bones.	**c. 3000** Use of copper spreads throughout Europe.	**c. 2500** The horse is domesticated in central Asia.
c. 1040 The Zhou conquer the Shang. **c. 650** Iron in use.	**c. 1600** Mycenaean civilization begins in Greece.	**c. 1500** The use of iron begins in Turkey. **c. 1200** The Jewish religion emerges.
221 Qin Shihuandgi, the First Emperor. **202** Han dynasty begins.	**510** The Roman republic is founded.	**c. 600–200** The Paracas culture in Peru. **c. 500** The Nok culture in West Africa.
A.D. 68 The Han emperor sends his ministers to India.	**A.D. 43** The Roman Empire invades Britain.	**A.D. 30** Death of Jesus Christ. Spread of Christianity begins.
584 Emperor Yang Di begins Great Canal. **618–906** The Tang dynasty rules.	**117** The Roman Empire is at its greatest extent.	**300s** The Ghanaian Empire is founded in West Africa.
627 Xuanzang leaves Xi'an for India. Wood-block printing is invented.	**c. 542** Bubonic plague spreads through Europe.	**622** Mohammed founds the religion of Islam in Arabia.
900–1000 Gunpowder is invented. The compass is used in navigation.	**959** The Unification of England.	**c. 900s** Arabs settle the east coast of Africa. **935** The text of the Quran is finished.
1271 Marco Polo leaves Venice for China. **1275** Marco Polo meets Kublai Khan.	**1066** The Normans conquer England.	**c. 1000** The Vikings colonize Greenland and travel to America.
1346 Ibn Battuta arrives in China. **1368** The Ming dynasty rules.	**1340s** The bubonic plague continues to spread through Europe.	**c. 1345–1530** The Aztec civilization. **1352** Ibn Battuta travels to Africa.
1405–33 Zheng He makes seven voyages to Southeast Asia, the Persian Gulf, and East Africa.	**1492** The first globe is made in Germany by Martin Behaim.	**1498** The Portuguese (led by Vasco da Gama) arrive in India.
1514 The first European sailors arrive in China from Portugal.	**1532** John Calvin starts the Protestant movement in France.	**1530s** The European slave trade begins across the Atlantic Ocean.
1582 The Jesuit priest Matteo Ricci arrives in China.	**1618** The Thirty Years War of religion starts.	**1607** The first English settlement is founded in America (Virginia).
1636 Xu Xiake begins his journey. **1644** The Qing dynasty rules.	**1667** The French begin to expand under Louis XIV.	**1680** The Rozvi empire in Zimbabwe.
1793 Lord Macartney travels to China.	**1756** The Seven Years War begins. **1789** The French Revolution begins.	**c. 1700s** European exploration of Africa. **1775–83** The American Revolution.
1839–42 The First Opium War. **1856–60** The Second Opium War.	**1807** The slave trade is abolished in Britain.	**1789** George Washington becomes the first president of the United States.
1911 The Qing dynasty ends. China becomes a republic. **1921** Chinese Communist Party founded.	**1884–85** The West African conference is held in Berlin (Germany).	**1857** The Indian Mutiny. **1861** The American Civil War begins.
1934 The Long March begins. **1937** Japanese troops invade China.	**1914-18** World War I.	**1915** Africa continues to be divided by foreign powers. **1917** The United States enters World War I.
1949 Chairman Mao establishes the People's Republic of China. **1966** The Cultural Revolution begins.	**1939-45** World War II.	**1941** The United States enters World War II.
1976 Chairman Mao dies. The Cultural Revolution ends.	**1961** The Berlin Wall is built in Germany.	**1961** John F. Kennedy becomes president of the United States. **1963** John F. Kennedy is assassinated.
1980s The Chinese government opens its doors to the West for the purposes of trade.	**1972** The European Community gains more members.	**1965–73** The United States is involved in the Vietnam War.
1989 Prodemocracy demonstrators are killed by the army in Tiananmen Square.	**1985** Mikhail Gorbachev becomes the leader of the Soviet Union.	**1981** Ronald Reagan becomes the U.S. president.
1990s China's economy expands rapidly. **1992** The first-ever state visit to China by a Japanese emperor.	**1989** Boris Yeltsin becomes leader of Russia. **1991** East and West Germany are united. The Berlin Wall is destroyed.	**1990** Nelson Mandela is released in South Africa. Apartheid begins to break apart. **1993** Bill Clinton becomes the U.S. president.

Glossary

A

afterlife: many people believe that when you die you are reborn into another world. This is called the afterlife.

allies: people who are united in a cause, such as a war, by an official agreement.

archaeologist: a person who studies the past by methodically **excavating** ancient sites and artifacts.

arranged marriage: a marriage that is arranged by people other than the bride and groom.

astronomy: the name given to the study of everything in the universe.

B

bronzes: a name for a sculpture, statue, or crafted object made of bronze.

C

calligraphy: beautiful handwriting that is thought of as an art form.

cartography: the name given to the practice of making maps.

celestial globe: a model of how the universe is thought to look.

colonies: lands claimed and controlled by a power outside their boundaries.

communes: groups of people who live together and share work and possessions.

D

dynasty: a series of related rulers.

E

envoy: a messenger or representative of a king or queen.

ethnic: the name given to groups of people who have things like race, religion, or language in common.

eunuch: a male servant who is castrated (has part of his reproductive organs removed so that he cannot have children) employed in many of the imperial households.

excavated: something that is dug up in a methodical and scientific manner.

exported: goods transported out of a country for sale abroad are exported.

G

geologist: someone who studies the structure and history of the earth.

grasslands: land (usually flat) where grass grows as the most common plant.

guerrilla: soldiers who do not belong to an official army. Guerrillas use different fighting tactics from national armies, usually involving ambushes and sabotage.

H

Huns: several **nomadic** tribes of Asia and eastern Europe.

I

Imperial concubine: the second or third wife of a Chinese emperor.

incentive: an extra reason to do something.

industrial: anything connected with the production of goods with technology.

inscriptions: a series of words or pictures carved or written onto a surface.

J

Jesuit: a member of the Roman Catholic Society of Jesus, founded by St. Ignatius in the 16th century. The Jesuits worked all over the world as **missionaries**.

K

Karl Marx: (1818–1883) a German writer who founded the political theory of Communism.

M

Manchu: an **ethnic** people who live in northeast China.

meditate: to think deeply for an extended time about one thing.

Mesopotamia: the area between the Euphrates and Tigris Rivers (modern-day Iraq). The civilizations of Sumer and Babylonia thrived in Mesopotamia.

millet: a grass that is grown for grain and to feed animals.

missionaries: people who try to convert people from one religion to another.

mountain sickness: an illness caused by lack of oxygen, which involves bad headaches, shortness of breath, and sickness.

Muslims: people who follow the religion of Islam founded by the prophet Mohammed in Arabia in A.D. 622. Muslims try to live their lives according to the teachings of the Quran, which they believe to be the words of God as heard by Mohammed.

N

Nationalist: beliefs held by people within a country that are based on that country's identity.

Neolithic: the period of history from 9000 to 6000 B.C. in southwest Asia and 4000 to 2400 B.C. in Europe. Neolithic people used stone tools to farm the land.

nomads: people who travel from place to place.

O

officials: people who have jobs in government.

opium: an addictive drug made by drying the juice of poppy seeds.

P

pagodas: beautifully decorated temples or towers, usually many stories high.

Persian: anything relating to the country of Persia. Persia changed its name to Iran in 1935.

physics: the study of energy and matter.

polo: a team game played on horseback.

pomegranates: the fruit of the pomegranate tree, which usually grows in **semitropical** areas of the world. Pomegranates are about the size of oranges and contain many red seeds.

porcelain: a fine hard ceramic mixture (fired clay) that is white in color.

Privy Council: the name of the group of officials who govern the country at the instruction of the emperor.

R

rationing: a ration is a set or restricted amount of something (usually food).

Red Guards: armylike units of young people who were taught to destroy anything connected with history during the Cultural Revolution.

S

saltpeter: one of the explosive ingredients of gunpowder.

Sanskrit: the ancient language of India.

scholar: a learned or well-educated person.

seals: stamps with personal names or official titles on them.

semitropical: places near, but not in, the tropics.

sulfur: a light-yellow powder that smells terrible and has many different uses in medicine and industry.

T

terra-cotta: unfired (or unbaked) clay.

textiles: material woven from spun threads.

treasury: the name for the government's or emperor's store of money, gold, or treasures.

Turks: people from Turkey (in southern Europe, next to Greece).

Z

zoologists: scientists who study animals.

Index

Numbers in **bold** indicate an illustration. Words in **bold** are in the glossary on page 47.